D1383416

Opuestos: Grande y pequeño

Opposites: Big and Little

Luana K. Mitten

Rourke
Publishing LLC
Vero Beach, Florida 32964

© 2009 Rourke Publishing LLC

All rights reserved. No part of this book may be reproduced or utilized in any form or by any means, electronic or mechanical including photocopying, recording, or by any information storage and retrieval system without permission in writing from the publisher.

www.rourkepublishing.com

PHOTO CREDITS: © Jaroslaw Wojcik: page 3 left; © Arthur Kwiatkowski: page 3 right; © Velychko: page 5; © Alexander Shalamov: page 6, 7; © Wouter van Caspel: page 8, 9; © Ng Yin Jian: page 10, 11; © viZualStudio: page 13; © Jessica Bopp: page 14, 15; © Frank B Yuwono: page 17; © jarvis gray: page 18, 19; © Vladimirs Prusakovs: page 21; © Jelani Memory : page 22, 23; ©

Editor: Kelli Hicks

Cover design by Nicola Stratford, bdpublishing.com

Interior Design by Heather Botto

Spanish Editorial Services by Cambridge BrickHouse, Inc.   www.cambridgebh.com

Library of Congress Cataloging-in-Publication Data

Mitten, Luana K.
  Opposites : big and little / Luana K. Mitten.
     p. cm. -- (Concepts)
  Learning the concept of opposites through riddles and poetry.
  ISBN 978-1-60472-417-2 (hardcover)
  ISBN 978-1-60472-813-2 (softcover)
  ISBN 978-1-60472-499-8 (hardcover bilingual)
  ISBN 978-1-60472-817-0 (softcover bilingual)
  1. English language--Synonyms and antonyms--Juvenile literature. I. Title.
  PE1591.M643 2008
  423'.1--dc22
                           2008018795

Printed in the USA
CG/CG

Rourke Publishing

www.rourkepublishing.com – rourke@rourkepublishing.com
Post Office Box 3328, Vero Beach, FL 32964

Grande y pequeño, pequeño y grande, ¿cuál es la diferencia entre grande y pequeño?

Big and little, little and big, what's the difference between big and little?

Para mi pez dorado, una pecera pequeña.

For my goldfish, a little fish tank.

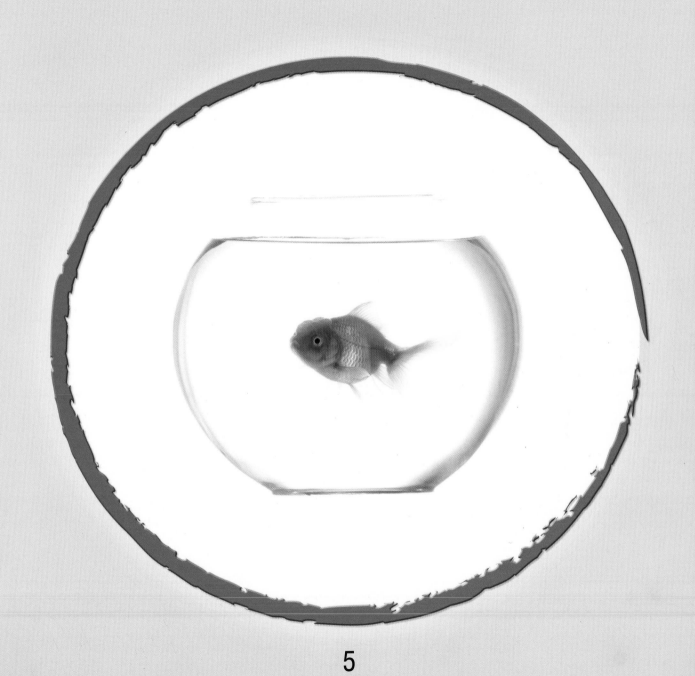

5

Para un tiburón, una pecera GRANDE.

For a shark, a BIG fish tank.

Para un avispón, un hueco pequeño.

For a hornet, a little hole.

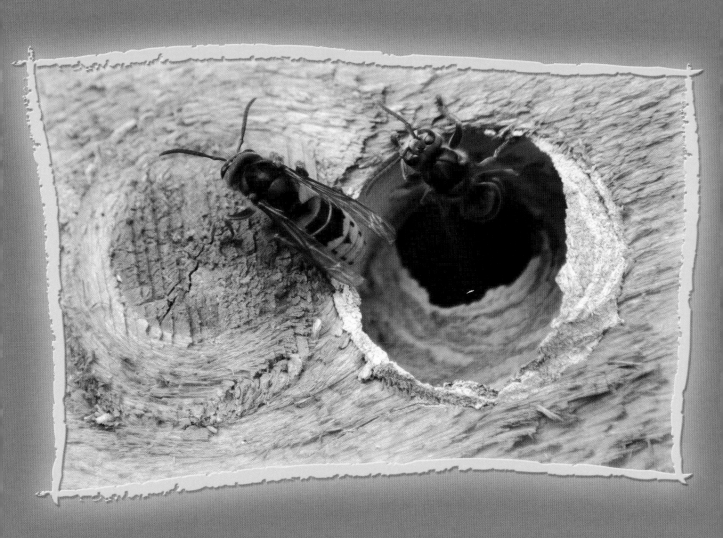

9

Para un conejo, un hueco GRANDE.

For a rabbit, a BIG hole.

Para un petirrojo, un nido pequeño.

For a robin, a little nest.

12

Para un azulejo, un nido pequeño.

For a bluebird, a little nest.

Para un águila, un nido GRANDE.

For an eagle, a BIG nest.

Para un cangrejo hermitaño, una concha pequeña.

For a hermit crab, a little shell.

17

Para una tortuga marina, un caparazón GRANDE.

For a sea turtle, a BIG shell.

Para un ratoncito, una casa pequeña.

For a mouse, a little house.

21

Para mí, ¡una casa GRANDE!

For me, a BIG house!

22

Índice / Index

Lecturas adicionales / Further Reading

Child, Lauren. *Charlie and Lola's Opposites.* 2007.
Ford, Bernette. Sorrentino, Christiano. *A Big Dog: An Opposites Book,* 2008.
Falk, Laine. *Let's Talk About Opposites: Morning to Night,* 2007.
Holland, Gina. *Soft and Hard (I Know My Opposites),* 2007.

Sitios web recomendados / Recommended Websites

www.abcteach.com/grammar/online/opposites1.htm
www.resources.kaboose.com/games/read1html
www.learn4good.com/kids/preschool_english_spanish_language_books.htm

Sobre la autora / About the Author

Luana Mitten y su familia viven en Tampa, Florida, donde les gusta montar en bicicleta. Luana y su esposo tienen bicicletas grandes y su hijo tiene una bicicleta pequeña.

Luana Mitten and her family live in Tampa, Florida where they like riding bikes. Luana and her husband have big bikes and her son has a little bike.

UNION COUNTY PUBLIC LIBRARY
316 E. Windsor St., Monroe, N.C. 28112